CASINO CRAPS
for the
WINNER

CASINO CRAPS
for the
WINNER

Avery Cardoza

CARDOZA PUBLISHING
Cardoza School of Blackjack ● Gambling Research Institute

To my grandparents
Fay and Louis   Ann and Irving

Printing History

First Printing	**August 1982**
Second Printing	**February 1983**
Third Printing	**July 1985**

CARDOZA PUBLISHING

Cardoza School of Blackjack ● Gambling Research Institute
P.O. Box 5267
Santa Cruz, CA 95063

ISBN: 0-9607618-1-0

Table of Contents

4

List of Tables and Charts

I. INTRODUCTION

Craps is the most exciting of the casino games for it offers the player opportunities to win large sums of money quickly. But big money can be lost just as fast unless the player has a basic knowledge of the bets available at craps and knows how to use them in a coordinated strategy. We'll teach you all the fundamentals of playing and winning so that once you've finished reading this book, you'll play confidently, and possess all the information necessary to be a winner.

You'll learn everything you'll ever need to know about craps — from the rules of the game, how to bet and how to play, to the combinations of the dice and the casino vocabulary. You'll learn the best bets to make and how to use them in winning strategies, and how to bankroll and handle your cash so that you'll manage your money like a pro.

We present winning strategies for players betting with and against the dice, and show the best ways conservative and aggressive players alike can bet their money while still maintaining the best chances of winning.

Our winning strategies are based on the soundest principles. By making use of only the best bets available to the player, we'll reduce the house edge to the barest minimum. In fact, the bulk of our money will be bet on the free-odds bets, wagers the house has no edge on whatsoever!

All our winning strategies contain built-in betting and money management techniques to make otherwise average wins into big wins, and to restrict losing sessions to affordable amounts. Not only will you learn to win, but you'll be shown how to protect your wins, so that when you leave the table, your wins will be in your pocket and not in your memory. In short, you'll be armed with the most powerful craps strategies available.

Whether you're a high roller betting $100 or $1,000 a throw or just a casual gambler betting $1 a play, you'll find *Casino Craps for the Winner* an indispensible guide to winning, and the only craps book you'll ever need to consult!

II. BEGINNER'S GUIDE TO CASINO CRAPS

The Table

The standard casino craps table is rectangular in shape and depending upon the particular size of the casino's table, is built to accommodate between 15 to 24 players. The sides of the table are several feet above the layout where the bets are made, giving the players an edge to lean on, and giving the dice walls to carom off.

The Layout

The craps layout is divided into three distinct sections. The two end sections, which are identical, are areas around which the players cluster, and where the majority of bets are made. Each end area is run by one of the standing dealers.

The middle area is flanked on either side by a boxman and stickman. This area contains the proposition, or center bets, and is completely under the jurisdiction of the stickman.

The layout is a large piece of green felt with various imprintations marking the plethora of bets possible. All action is centered on the layout. Bets are placed, paid off and collected on this felt surface. And, of course, it is on the layout where the dice are thrown.

Layouts in Northern Nevada, Atlantic City and Downtown Las Vegas casinos are basically the same, though some clubs may have slight variations. Some Las Vegas Strip casinos have slight differences as well, but none of these need concern us, for the game of craps is basically the same whatever casino you play in. The minor variations that do occur, concern bets whose odds are so poor that we wouldn't want to make them anyway.

The Dice

The game of craps is played with two standard six sided dice, with each die numbered from 1 to 6. The dice are manufactured so that they fall as randomly as possible, with a 5 being just as likely to fall on one die as a 3. However, we'll see later that combining two dice together creates some combinations that are more likely to appear than others, and this is the basis of the odds in craps.

Players

Only one player is needed to play craps, while as many as can fit around a craps table are the maximum.

Table 1
The Layout

Casino Personnel

The average craps table is manned by a crew of four casino employees — one stickman, who stands at the center of the table, two dealers, who stand on the opposite side of the stickman at either end of the table, and a boxman who is seated between the two standing dealers and directly across from the stickman.

Let's look at the function of each crewman in turn.

The Stickman

The stickman's main responsibility is the handling of the dice, a task he performs with a flexible, hooked stick. When a new shooter is coming-out, the stickman will offer him a cache of dice to choose from, and after two have been selected, will return the remaining dice to his box.

After each roll of the dice, the stickman will announce the number thrown, and bring the dice back to the center of the table. Usually, he will supply additional information about its consequences.

If a 7 is thrown on the come-out roll, he may announce, "7, winner on the pass line."

If instead, a 2, 3 or 12 is rolled on the come-out, he may say, "Craps, line away."

When a shooter sevens-out, the stickman might exclaim, "7 out, line away."

A good stickman is a show in himself, and by the excitement he generates, makes the game more lively and colorful for both the players and the dealers. And from the casino's standpoint, happy players tend to bet heavier and wilder than they normally would.

The dice will be returned to the shooter after the dealers have finished making payoffs.

The stickman is also responsible for the proposition, or center bets made in the middle of the layout. He will place all proposition bets directed his way into their proper location on the layout.

If these bets are winners, the stickman will direct the dealers to pay off the winning players, and if the bets are losers, he will collect the lost bets and push them over to the boxman.

The Dealers

There is a dealer located on either side of the boxman, and his main responsibility is to handle all the monetary transactions and betting on his end of the table. He pays off winning bets and collects losing ones, converts cash into chips, and will change chips into higher or lower denominations for the player.

Though the player can make many of the bets himself, there are wagers such as the place bets and certain free-odds bets which must be given to the dealer to be placed.

Each standing dealer has a **marker buck**, a plastic disk used to indicate the established point. If a player is coming-out, beginning his roll, the marker buck will be lying on its black side, labeled "Off," and if a point is established, the dealer will flip the marker buck to the white side, marked "On," and place it in the appropriately numbered box to indicate the point.

It is with the dealers that the player will have most of his contact and to whom he can address his questions.

The Boxman

The boxman sits between the two dealers and across from the stickman, and from this central position, supervises the running of the craps table. His job is not only to watch over the casinos bankroll, most of which sits right in front of him in huge stacks, but to make sure the dealers make the correct payoffs so that neither the player nor the house gets shorted.

He is responsible for settling any disputes that may arise between the players and the dealers. Generally, the benefit of the doubt will be given to the player on any disputed call.

If the dice leave the table for any reason, the returned dice are brought directly to the boxman for inspection. He will check the logo and coded numbers on the dice to make sure they haven't been switched, and will inspect the surfaces for imperfections that may influence the game. If, for any reason, the boxman feels suspicious of the returned dice, he will remove them from play and have the stickman offer the shooter a new pair.

When one boxman is on duty, he will supervise one end of the table while the stickman watches the other.

However, when the action is fast, and stacks of chips are riding on each roll of the dice, a second boxman will often be added to the crew to help watch the table. In these cases, the boxmen will sit next to each other behind the chips, each being responsible for one end of the table.

In addition to the boxmen, there are other supervisors, called floormen and pit bosses, who watch over the action from behind the boxman in the area known as the pit.

The Pit

Craps tables are arranged in a pattern so that a central area, known as the **pit**, is formed in the middle. The tables are arranged around the pit so that the boxmen and standing dealers have their backs to the pit area, and so that the floormen, standing inside the pit, can easily watch over all of the craps tables.

Floormen

The floormen spend their entire shift on their feet, and are responsible for supervising a particular table or group of tables in the pit.

In addition to these supervisory capacities, they deal with players that have established credit lines. If a player requests credit, the floorman will check to see if his credit is good, and if verified, will authorize the dealer to give the player the requested chips. At the same time, or soon afterwards, he will bring the player an IOU to sign, acknowledging the credit transaction.

The Pit Boss

The pit boss, under whose authority the floormen work, is in charge of the entire craps pit. He's rarely in contact with the players, unless a high roller is playing, whereby he may come over and introduce himself or offer the roller some comps (freebies).

Entering a Game

To enter a craps game, slip into a space by the rail of the craps table. After catching the dealer's attention, place your cash on the layout and inform him of the denomination of chips you would like. The dealer will take your money, and give it to the boxman who will supervise the exchange.

Converting Traveller's Checks and Money Orders to Cash

The dealers will accept only cash or chips at the table, so if you bring traveller's checks, money orders or the like, you must go to the area of the casino marked **Casino Cashier** to get these converted to cash. Be sure to bring proper identification to insure a smooth transaction.

Casino Chips

Chip denominations run in $1, $5, $25, $100 and $500 units. $1 chips are generally referred to as **silver**, $5 chips as **nickels**, $25 chips as **quarters**, and $100 chips as **dollars**. Unless playing at a 25¢ minimum craps table, dollar units are the minimum currency available.

Bets

Casinos prefer that the player uses chips for betting purposes, for the handling of money at the tables is cumbersome and slows the game. However, cash can be used to bet with, though all payoffs will be in chips.

House Limits

The house limits will be posted on placards located on each corner of the table. They will indicate the minimum bet required to play and also the maximum bet allowed.

Minimum bets range from $1 and $5 per bet, to a maximum of $500, $1000 or $2,000 a bet. Occasionally, 25¢ minimum craps tables may be found as well. If special arrangements are made, a player can bet as much as he can muster in certain casinos. The Horseshoe Casino in Las Vegas advertises that it will book any bet, no matter the size. In 1981, a man walked into the Horseshoe and placed a bet for $777,777. He bet the don't pass, and walked out two rolls later with one and a half million dollars in cash!

Converting Chips into Cash

Dealers do not convert your chips into cash. Once you've bought your chips at the table, that cash is dropped into a dropbox, and thereafter unobtainable at the table. When you are ready to convert your chips, take them to the cashier's cage where they'll be changed into cash.

Free Drinks and Cigarettes

Casinos offer their customers unlimited free drinking while gambling at the tables. In addition to alcoholic beverages, a player can order milk, soft drinks, juices or any other beverages. This is ordered through and served by a cocktail waitress.

Cigarettes and cigars are also complimentary and can be ordered through the cocktail waitress.

Tipping

Tipping, or toking, as it is called in casino parlance, should be viewed as a gratuitous gesture by the player to the crew of dealers he feels has given him good service. Toking is totally at the player's discretion, and in no way should be considered an obligation.

If you toke, toke only when you're winning, and only if the crew is friendly and helpful to you. Do not toke dealers that you don't like or ones that try to make you feel guilty about not tipping. Dealers that make playing an unpleasant experience for you deserve nothing.

Tips are shared by the crew working the craps table. Though the usual tip is to make a proposition bet, with the exclamation "one for the boys," a better way to toke the crew would be to make a line bet for them, so they can have a good chance of winning the bet. Dealers prefer this type of tip for they too are aware how poor the proposition bets are. This is also better than just handing over the toke, for if the bet is won, the dealer wins double for the tip — the amount bet for him plus the winnings from that bet.

Play of the Game and the Come-Out Roll

When a new player is to throw the dice, the stickman will empty his box of dice and push them across the layout with his stick. This player, known as the **shooter**, selects two dice of his choice, and the stickman will retrieve the remaining dice and return them to his box. In a new game, the player closest to the boxman's left side will receive the dice first, and the rotation of the dice will go clockwise from player to player around the craps table.

The shooter has no advantage over the other players except perhaps the psychological edge he may get throwing the dice himself. He is required to make either a pass or don't pass bet as the shooter, and in addition, can make any other bets allowed.

There are a wide variety of bets the players can make, and these bets should be placed before the shooter throws the dice. Players can bet with the dice or against them at their preference, but in either case, the casino will book all wagers.

Play is ready to begin. The shooter is supposed to throw the dice so that they bounce off the far wall of the table. If the throw does not reach the far wall, the shooter will be requested to toss harder on his next throw, and if he persists in underthrowing the dice, the boxman may disallow him from throwing further. This policy protects against cheats that can manipulate unobstructed throws of the dice.

The first throw is called the **come-out** roll, and is the most significant roll in craps. It marks the first roll of a **shoot**, and can either become an automatic winner or loser for players betting with the dice, called **right bettors**, or those betting against the dice, called **wrong bettors**, or establish a point with which the shooter hopes to repeat before a 7 is thrown.

The come-out roll works as follows. The throw of a 7 or 11 on the come-out roll is an automatic winner for the pass line bettors, players betting that the dice will win, or pass, while the throw of a **craps**, a 2, 3 or 12 is an automatic loser. For the don't pass bettors, those betting against the dice, the come-out roll works almost exactly opposite to the pass line bet. A come-out roll of a 7 or an 11 is an automatic loser, a 2 or a 3 an automatic winner, while the 12 (in some casinos a 2 instead) is a standoff.

If the come-out roll is an automatic decision, a 2, 3, 7, 11 or 12, the affected players will have their bets paid or collected, and the following roll will be a new come-out roll.

Any other number thrown, a 4, 5, 6, 8, 9 or 10, becomes the **point**, and the dealers will indicate this by flipping their respective marker bucks to the white side marked *on*, and move the disk into the rectangular numbered boxes corresponding to the point number thrown.

The shoot will continue until either the point is repeated, a winner for the pass line bettors and a loser for the don't pass bettors, or until a seven is thrown, known as **sevening-out**, a loser on the pass line and winner on the don't pass. In either case, the shoot will have been completed, and the following roll will be a new come-out roll, the start of a new shoot.

Once a point is established, only the 7 and the point are consequential rolls for the pass and don't pass bettors, also called **line bettors**. All other rolls are neutral throws for these bets.

There are many other bets available to the player as we will discuss later, some that can be made only after a point is established, and others that can be made at any time during a shoot. So while the line bettors may not be affected by a particular throw, the dealers may be paying off or collecting chips on other affected wagers while the shoot is in progress.

The shooter can continue throwing the dice until he sevens-out, whereupon, after all the bets are settled on the layout, the stickman will present his collection of dice to the next player in a clockwise rotation. Even though the shooter may crap-out (the throw of a 2, 3 or 12) on his come-out roll, a losing roll for the pass line bettors, the shooter does not have to yield the dice. It is only when the shooter throws a 7 before his point repeats, sevens-out, that the dice must be relinquished.

The Come-Out Roll Capsulated
The come-out roll occurs when:

1 —A new shooter takes the dice.

2 —The shooter throws a 2, 3, 7, 11 or 12 on the come-out roll, an automatic winner or loser for the line bettors.

3 —After a point is established, the shooter either repeats that point or sevens-out.

Betting Right or Wrong
Betting right or wrong are only casino terms used to designate whether a player is betting with the dice, betting right, or betting against the dice, betting wrong, and are in no way indicative of a correct or incorrect way of playing. As we shall see, both ways of betting are equally valid.

III. UNDERSTANDING THE ODDS

Knowing how to figure the possible combinations that can occur when two dice are thrown is essential to understanding the basics of craps — the bets, the odds and the payoffs. You'll be surprised at how simple the odds really are, and will find craps to be a more rewarding experience once you learn these fundamentals.

Craps is played with two dice, individually called **die**, and each die is a near perfect six sided cube, guaranteed to be within 1/10,000 of an inch accurate.

Each die has six equally possible outcomes when thrown — numbers one through six. The two dice thrown together have a total of 36 possible outcomes, the six combinations of one die by the six combinations of the other. The chart below shows these combinations. Notice how certain totals have more possibilities of being thrown, or are more *probable* of occurring by the random throw of the two dice.

14

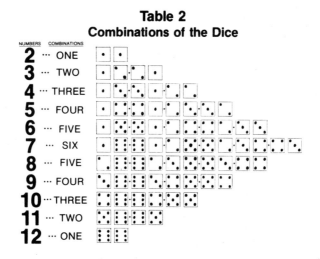

Table 2
Combinations of the Dice

You can see by the chart that the 7 is more likely to be thrown than any other number, having six possible combinations. Next in frequency are the 6 and the 8, five outcomes each, then the 5 and the 9, four outcomes, the 4 and the 10, three outcomes apiece, the 3 and the 11, two outcomes, and finally, the 2 and the 12, one combination each.

A Shortcut to Remembering the Odds

Notice the symmetry of combinations on either side of the 7. The 6 and 8 have equal possibilities of being thrown, just as the 5 and 9, 4 and 10, 3 and 11, and 2 and 12 do.

If you take rolls of 7 and below and subtract one from that number, you arrive at the correct number of combinations for that roll. Thus, there are four ways to roll a 5 (5-1), six ways to roll a 7 (7-1) and one way to roll a 2 (2-1).

For numbers greater than the 7, match that number with the corresponding symmetrical number on the other side of the 7, and subtract one. Thus, to find the combinations of the 8, you match it with the 6 (which has an equal likelihood of occurring), and subtracting one, you get five combinations.

Figuring the Odds of Rolling a Specific Number

To figure the odds of rolling any particular number, divide the number of combinations for that particular number into 36, the total number of combinations possible.

Let's say the 7. There are six ways to roll a 7. Dividing the six combinations into 36, the total number of combinations, we find the odds of rolling a 7 on any one roll is one in six (6/36 reduced to

1/6), or equivalently, 5 to 1. The chart below shows the odds of rolling a number on any one roll.

Chart 3
Odds of Rolling the Numbers

	Combinations	Chance of Being Rolled	Expressed in Odds
2 or 12	1	1/36	35 to 1
3 or 11	2	2/36	17 to 1
4 or 10	3	3/36	11 to 1
5 or 9	4	4/36	8 to 1
6 or 8	5	5/36	6.2 to 1
7	6	6/36	5 to 1

The listing of two numbers together such as the 5 or 9, is done to abbreviate. The odds apply to either the 5 or the 9, not to both together.

Understanding the Terminology —
Correct Odds, House Payoff and Edge

The **house advantage** or **edge** is the difference between the player's chances of winning the bet, called the **correct odds**, and the casino's actual payoff, called the **house payoff** or simply, the **payoff**. For example, the correct odds of rolling a 7 are 5 to 1. Since the house will payoff only 4 to 1 should the 7 be thrown, they maintain an edge of 16.67 percent on this wager.

To pay craps intelligently and better understand the choices available to him, the player must first and foremost be aware of the house advantage on every bet he will ever make, for that, in the long run, determines the player's chances of winning.

Five for One, Five to One

Sometimes on a layout you will see payoffs represented as *for* instead of the usual *to*, such as 9 for 1. This means that the payoff will be a total of nine units, eight winning chips along with your original bet, a house subterfuge to increase its edge over the player. The usual 9 to 1 payoff means nine winning chips and your original bet returned, for a total of 10 units.

Beware of any payoffs with the *for*. As a rule, this type of bet has poor odds to begin with and we wouldn't want to make it anyway, with the *to* or the *for*.

IV. The Bets

Craps offers the player a wide variety of possible wagers, with each bet having its own characteristics and inherent odds. Some bets, which we will refer to as **sequence** bets, may require a series of rolls before the outcome is determined, while the outcome of others, called **one-roll** bets, is determined on the very next roll.

Some bets are paid off by the house at even-money, for every dollar wagered, the player wins a dollar, while other bets have payoffs as high as 30 to 1. However, as you will see, generally the higher the house payoff, the worse the odds are for the player.

And the odds of the bet, that is, the mathematical house return on every dollar wagered, is the most important concern of the player. To have the best chances of winning, the player must avoid all the sucker bets, and make only the best bets available to him.

A. Most Advantageous Bets

The bets presented in this section have the lowest built-in house edge of all the bets in craps, and one bet, the free-odds bet, gives the house no advantage whatsoever. These bets, the pass, don't pass, come, don't come and the free-odds bets, are the most important bets a player can make, and are the foundation of the winning strategies.

The Line Bets — Pass and Don't Pass

These even-money bets can only be made on a come-out roll, before a point is established, and give the house an edge of only 1.4 percent. And when backed by the free-odds wagers, the overall house edge drops to 0.8 percent in a single odds game and to 0.6 percent in a double odds game.

Pass Line

Players making pass line bets are wagering that the dice will pass, or win, and are called right bettors. Pass line bets are also referred to as **front line** bets, and are made by placing the wager in the area marked *pass line*.

On the come-out roll, a throw of a 7 or 11 is an automatic winner for the pass line bettors while the throw of a craps, a 2, 3 or 12 is an automatic loser. If any other number is thrown, the 4, 5, 6, 8, 9 or 10, then that number is established as the point, and the shooter must repeat the point before a 7 is thrown for pass line bettors to win. The throw of a 7 before the point repeats is a loser for pass line bettors, called sevening-out, and the dealers will collect the lost bets.

Once the point is established, only the 7 and the point number affect the pass line bettor. All other numbers have no bearing on the bet and can be considered neutral throws.

Let's look at three progressions to see how the pass line bet works.

1 —The come-out roll is a 5, establishing 5 as the point. The following roll is a 2, a neutral throw, for a point has already been established. An 8 is then thrown, still having no bearing on the outcome, and then a 5. The point was repeated, or **made**, before the seven was thrown, and the pass line bettors win their bets.

2 —The come-out roll is a 7, an automatic winner for the pass line bettors, and they are paid off by the dealers. Since the progression has been completed, the following roll will be another come-out roll.

3 —Here is a losing proposition. The come-out roll is a 9, establishing 9 as the point. The shooter then rolls a 6, then a 12, and then an 11. All three rolls are neutral since a point is already established. The following roll is a 7. Since the 7 was rolled before the 9, the shooter's point repeated, pass line bettors lose and the dealers will collect their bets. A new come-out roll will ensue.

Pass Line Capsulated

Payoff: Even-Money   House Edge: 1.4%
Automatic Winners — 7 or 11 on the come-out roll.
Automatic Losers — 2, 3 or 12 on the come-out roll.
If a point is established on the come-out roll, the pass line bettor:
Wins by the point repeating before the 7 is thrown.
Loses by the roll of a 7 before the point repeats.

Don't Pass

Players betting don't pass are called wrong bettors, and are betting against the dice. Don't pass bets are also called **back line** bets and are made by placing the wager in the area marked *don't pass*.

On the come-out roll, a throw of a 2 or 3 is an automatic winner for the don't pass bettors, while a 7 or an 11 is an automatic loser. The 12 is a standoff between the back line bettor and the house. (In some casinos the 2 is the standoff and the 12 is the automatic winner. Either way it makes no difference, for there is only one way to throw the 2 or 12.)

Once the point is established, don't pass bettors win by having the 7 thrown before the shooter repeats his point, and lose by the point being repeated before the shooter sevens-out. Here are some progressions to illustrate the don't pass wager.

1 —The come-out roll is a 6, establishing 6 as the point. The following

rolls are a 5 (no bearing on the outcome), then a 12 (still no bearing) and then a 7. Since the 7 was rolled before the 6 repeated, don't pass bettors win.

2 —The come-out roll is a 3, an automatic winner for the don't pass bettor.

3 —The come-out roll is a 4, establishing 4 as the point. A 3 is then rolled (neutral), and then a 4, a loss for the back line bettors since the point repeated before the 7 was rolled.

Don't Pass Line Capsulated

Payoff: Even-Money   House Edge: 1.4 %
Automatic Winners — 2 (or 12) and 3 on the come-out roll.
Automatic Losers — 7 or 11 on the come-out roll.
Standoff — 12 (or 2 in some casinos) on the come-out roll.
If a point is established on the come-out roll don't pass bettors:
Win by the throw of a 7 before the point repeats.
Lose by the point repeating before the 7 is thrown.

Come and Don't Come Bets

The come and don't come bets work according to the same rules as the pass and don't pass bets except that the come and don't come bets can only be made once a point is established. The line bets, on the other hand, can only be placed on a come-out roll, before a point is established.

The advantage of these bets are that they allow the player to cover more points as a right or wrong bettor at the same low 1.4% house edge. And like the line bets, the overall house edge drops to 0.8% when backed by single odds, and 0.6% when backed by double odds.

Come bets are made by putting the chips into the area marked *come*, while don't come bets are placed in the *don't come* box. Won bets are paid at even-money.

Come Bets

We follow the play of the come bets just as we would with the pass line bets. A 7 or 11 on the first throw following the placing of the bet is an automatic winner, while a 2, 3 or 12 is an automatic loser.

Any other number thrown, the 4, 5, 6, 8, 9 or 10, becomes the point for that come bet, called the **come point**, and the dealer will move the bet from the come box into the large rectangular numbered boxes located at the top of the layout to mark the come point.

Once the come point is established, the bet is won if the come point repeats before the shooter sevens-out, and lost if the 7 is rolled before the point repeats. All other throws are inconsequential on this bet. Won bets will be paid off and removed from the layout.

The bettor can make continuous come bets until all the points are covered if he desires. Thus, it is possible for the throw of a 7 to simultaneously wipe out several established come bets. On the other hand, a hot shooter rolling point numbers can bring frequent winners to the aggressive come bettor.

Let's follow a progression where the right bettor makes both pass line and come bets.

Player Bets: $5 on the pass line.
The come-out roll is a 5, establishing 5 as the point.

Player Bets: $5 on the come.
The roll is an 8, establishing 8 as the come point. The dealer moves the $5 come bet to the rectangular box marked *8* to indicate that 8 is the point for that come bet. In effect, the player has two points working, the 5 and the 8, and decides to make another come bet.

Player Bets: $5 on the come.
The roll is a 6. The dealer moves this new come bet to the 6, the come point for this bet. The other two points are not affected by this roll.

Player Bets: The player has three points established, the 5, 6 and 8, and makes no more bets at this time.
The roll is a 5, a $5 winner on the pass line. It is paid off and removed from the layout, leaving the player with two come points, the 6 and 8.

Player Bets: $5 on the pass line. Since the next roll is a come-out roll and the player wants to cover another point, he bets the pass.
The roll is a 10, establishing 10 as the point.

Player Bets: No additional bets at this time.
The roll is a 2 (neutral on all established bets), then an 8 is thrown, a $5 winner on the come point of 8, and that bet is paid off and removed. The following roll is not a come-out roll, for the come point was made, not the pass line point, the 10.

Player Bets: Wishing to establish a third point, $5 is bet on the come.
The roll is a 7. While the 7 is a $5 winner for the new come bet, it is a loser for the two established points, and they are removed from the layout by the dealer.
The roll of the 7 cleared the layout, and the following roll will be a new come-out roll.

Don't Come Bets

Like the don't pass wager, a 7 or 11 on the first roll following a don't come bet is an automatic loser and the 2 and 3 are automatic winners, 12 being a standoff. (In casinos where the 2 is a standoff and the 12 a winner on the don't pass, the same will hold true for the don't come bets.)

If the 4, 5, 6, 8, 9 or 10 is thrown, establishing a point for that don't come bet, the dealer will move the chips behind the appropriate point box to mark the don't come point. Don't come bettors now win by having the 7 thrown before that point is made. Other numbers, as with the don't pass bets, are neutral rolls. Only the 7 and the come point determine the bet.

Let's follow a progression where the wrong bettor makes both don't pass and don't come bets.

Player Bets: $5 on the don't pass.
The roll is a 10, establishing 10 as the point.

Player Bets: Continuing to bet against the dice, the player now makes a $5 bet on the don't come.
The roll is a 2, a $5 winner on the new don't come bet, and that bet is paid off and removed.

Player Bets: $5 on the don't come.
The roll is a 6. The dealer moves the bet from the don't come area to the upper section of the box numbered 6 to indicate that 6 is the point for this don't come bet. The player now has two points working, the 10 and 6, and decides to establish a third point.

Player Bets: $5 on the don't come.
The roll is a 10, a $5 loser on the don't pass, since the point repeated before a 7 was thrown. The don't come point of 6 is unaffected, and the new don't come bet is moved to the 10 box, since 10 is the come point for the new don't come wager.

Player Bets: The player decides not to make any more bets, being content with his bets on points 6 and 10, and unwilling to place more bets on the layout. If he were to make another bet against the dice, he would bet don't pass for the next throw is a come-out roll.
The roll is a 7, a winner on both established come points, and they are paid off and removed. The next roll will be a new come-out roll.

Free-Odds Bets

Though not indicated anywhere on the layout, the free-odds bets are the best bets a player can make at craps, and are an indispensible part of the winning strategies. The free-odds bets are so named, for, unlike the other bets at craps, the house has no advantage over the player. Hence, the term free-odds.

However, to make a free-odds bet, the player must first have placed a pass, don't pass, come or don't come wager, and in a sense, is backing those bets, for the free-odds bet can only be made in conjunction with these wagers. When backed by single odds, the overall odds of the pass, don't pass, come and don't come bets drop to 0.8%, and where double odds are allowed and utilized, the overall odds drop to only 0.6% against the player. These are the best odds a player can get at craps.

Free-Odds — Pass Line

Once a point is established on the come-out roll, the pass line bettor is allowed to make an additional bet, called a free-odds bet, that his point will be repeated before a 7 is thrown. This bet is paid off at the correct odds, giving the house no edge, and is made by placing the chips behind the pass line wager and just outside the pass line area.

When single odds are allowed, the player can bet up to the amount wagered on his pass line bet, and in certain instances, he can bet more. And when double odds are allowed, the player can bet twice his pass line bet as a free-odds wager.

Though the player can bet less than the permissible amount on the free-odds wager and is allowed to reduce or remove this bet at any time, he should never do so, for the free-odds bets are the most advantageous bets in craps, and should be fully taken advantage of.

Following is a table which shows the correct odds of the point repeating before a 7 is thrown and the house payoff. Note how the house takes no percentage advantage on these bets since the payoff is identical to the correct odds.

Chart 4
Odds of Point Repeating Before a Seven

Point Number	Correct Odds	House Payoff
4 or 10	2 to 1	2 to 1
5 or 9	3 to 2	3 to 2
6 or 8	6 to 5	6 to 5

The odds presented in this table are easy to figure for the only numbers that affect the free-odds bet are the point number, which is a winner, and the 7, which is a loser. All other throws are inconsequential.

There are three ways to roll a winning 4 or 10, and six ways to roll a losing 7, thus 2 to 1 is the correct odds on points 4 or 10. A 5 or 9 can be rolled four ways each against the same six ways of rolling a 7, thus the correct odds are 3 to 2 against the 5 or 9. A 6 or 8 can be made by five combinations, and again, since there are six ways to roll a losing 7, the correct odds are 6 to 5 against the 6 or 8.

Special Allowances — Single Odds Game

To make the payoffs easier, most casinos will allow the player to make a single odds bet greater than his pass line (or come) bet in the following instances.

a. With a pass line bet such as $5 or $25 and the point being a 5 or 9, the casino will allow the player to make an odds bet of $6 and $30 respectively behind the line. If the bet is won, the 3 to 2 payoff on the $6 free-odds bet would be $9, and on the $30 bet, $45. If the player wasn't allowed this special allowance, he would be unable to get the full correct odds on the $5 or $25 free-odds bet since the $1 or more minimum craps tables do not deal in half dollars.

b. With a three unit bet such as $3 or $15, and the point being a 6 or 8, the casino will allow a five unit free-odds bet behind the line. This allows the player to take full advantage of the 6 to 5 payoff on points 6 and 8. In the above examples, $5 and $25 free-odds bets would be permitted, and if won, would pay the player $6 and $30 respectively.

A three unit bet translates to $3 for the $1 bettor, $15 for the $5 bettor, $30 for the $10 bettor, and so on. Any bet that can be divisible by three can be considered a three unit bet and be backed by the special allowance single odds bets. A $30 bet on the pass line can be backed by only $30 if the point is a 5 or 9 since the 3 to 2 payoff can be made on this amount, but if the point is a 6 or an 8, can be backed by $50 (five unit special allowance).

If uncertain about the amounts you are allowed to back your

pass line bet with, check with the dealer, and he will let you know the permissible wager.

Chart 5
Three Unit Bet - Single Odds Special Allowance Chart

Basic Three Unit Bet	6 or 8 as Point
$3	$5 ($6)
$15	$25 ($30)
$30	$50 ($60)
$45	$75 ($90)
$75	$125 ($150)
$300	$500 ($600)

The first column, Basic Three Unit Bet, is what our standard pass and come bet is, while the second column shows the special allowance permitted when the point is 6 or 8. Numbers in parenthesis indicate the amount paid if the single odds bet is won.

Note that this is only a partial listing of the basic three unit bets, and many more are possible for the player that wants to bet in different ranges than shown.

No special allowances are allowed for the 4 or 10 as points because they are easily paid off at 2 to 1 no matter what amount is wagered.

On bets smaller than $5 with the point being a 6 or 8, single odds bets will not be able to receive the full 6 to 5 payoff, and will be paid off at even-money only, for again, the craps tables do not stock units smaller than $1 chips.

On bets larger than $5 but in unequal multiples of $5, the free-odds bet will be paid to the highest multiple of $5 at 6 to 5, and the remainder will be paid at even-money. Thus, a $12 odds bet on the 8 will yield a payoff of only $14, $12 on the first $10 (at 6 to 5), and even-money on the unequal remainder of $2.

When the free-odds bets do not receive their full payoff, the bet works to the disadvantage of the player. Therefore, we recommend that pass and come wagers be made in multiples of $3, for this allows the player to take full advantage of the special allowances and lowers the overall house edge for the single odds game below 0.8 percent.

Double Odds - Pass Line

Double odds work just like single odds except that the player is allowed to bet double his pass line bet as a free-odds wager. If $10 was bet on the pass line and a 5 was established as the point, the double odds game would allow the player to bet $20 as a free-odds wager and receive the same correct 3 to 2 odds on that point, instead of only being allowed a $10 free-odds bet as in the single odds game.

When combined with the pass line bet, double odds brings the overall house edge down to only 0.6%, the best odds a player can get at craps. Therefore, when there is a choice of playing a single or double odds game, choose the latter, for you should take advantage of every favorable option allowed.

If you're uncertain whether double odds are allowed, just ask the dealer, and he will let you know. Most Reno casinos allow double odds as well as many of the Las Vegas clubs. At this time, Atlantic City casinos offer only single odds games, and Lake Tahoe is also predominately single odds.

Special Allowances - Double Odds Game

One special allowance to keep in mind on the double odds game. With a two unit bet on the pass line and the point a 6 or 8, double odds casinos will allow the player to wager five units as a free-odds bet. Thus, with a $10 bet ($5 unit chips), and the point a 6 or 8, a $25 double odds bet would be allowed. If won, the 6 to 5 payoff would bring $30 in winnings (six $5 chips, an easier payoff for the casino).

We recommend that the player bet in multiples of two for it permits us to take advantage of the special five unit allowance when the point is a 6 or an 8. Any bet that can be divisible by two can be considered as a two unit bet and be backed by the special five unit allowance if the point is a 6 or an 8.

Chart 6
Two Unit Bet - Double Odds Special Allowance Chart
Double Odds Allowed

*Basic Two Unit Bet	6 or 8 as Point	4, 5, 9 or 10 as Point
$2	$5 ($6)	$4
$10	$25 ($30)	$20
$20	$50 ($60)	$40
$30	$75 ($90)	$60
$50	$125 ($150)	$100
$200	$500 ($600)	$400

* This column, Basic Two Unit Bet, is what our standard pass and come bets will be. The third column is the normal double odds allowance for points 4, 5, 9 and 10.

Numbers in parenthesis indicate the amount paid if the double odds bet is won (at 6 to 5 payoff).

Other two unit bets are possible. These are just some examples.

Let's follow a sample sequence to see how the free-odds bet

works in a single odds game.

$15 is bet on the pass line, and the come-out roll is a 6. Taking advantage of the special five unit allowance, $25 is wagered as a free-odds bet behind the line. (This bet is played by the player.) If the shooter throws a 7 before the point repeats, the player would lose the $15 pass bet and the $25 free-odds bet, but should the point be rolled before the 7, $15 will be won on the pass line bet and $30 on the odds bet ($25 paid at 6 to 5).

If the game was a double odds game, the player could have backed the $15 pass bet with a $30 free-odds bet. And if the point was a 6, the free-odds bet would pay $36 if won ($30 at 6 to 5).

Free-Odds - Don't Pass

Once the point is established, don't pass bettors are allowed to make a free-odds bet that a 7 will be rolled before the point repeats. The bet is paid off at correct odds, the house enjoying no edge, and is made by placing the free-odds bet next to the don't pass wager in the don't pass box.

Since the odds favor the don't pass bettor once the point is established, there being more ways to roll a winning 7 than any point number, the don't pass bettor must *lay* odds, that is, put more money on the free-odds bet than he will win.

Let's say the point is a 4. The don't pass bettor's chances of winning the bet are now 2 to 1 in his favor. There are only three ways to roll a 4, a loser, against the six combinations of a 7, a winner. Therefore, the don't pass bettor must bet $20 to win $10 when the point is a 4 (or 10).

(On the other side of the bet, pass line bettors are receiving 2 to 1 odds, for their bet is the underdog, having only three winning chances against six losing combinations.)

To lay odds as a don't pass bettor, the allowable free-odds bet is determined by the *payoff*, not the original bet. Using the above example of a $10 bet on the don't pass with 4 established as the point, the don't pass bettor in a single odds game is allowed up to a $10 win on the free-odds bet. Since the odds are 2 to 1 in his favor, the don't pass bettor must lay $20 to win $10. If it was a double odds game, meaning the player could win $20 on his original $10 bet, than at 1 to 2 odds, $40 would have to be staked for a potential win of $20.

The odds the don't pass bettor must lay are exactly opposite the odds pass line bettors take on the same points. Below is a table showing the free-odds bets from the wrong bettors position.

Chart 7
Odds of Rolling a Seven Before Point Repeats

Point Number	Correct Odds	House Payoff
4 or 10	1 to 2	1 to 2
5 or 9	2 to 3	2 to 3
6 or 8	5 to 6	5 to 6

Note how the house has no percentage advantage on these bets since the payoff is identical to the correct odds.

Like the free-odds bets for right bettors, don't pass free-odds wagers can be removed or reduced at any time, but since these are the player's best bets, it should not be done.

Let's look at a sequence to see how the free-odds bet works for the don't pass bettor.

$10 is bet on the don't pass, and the come-out roll is a 9. The wrong bettor bets $15 behind the line as a free-odds bet, the maximum allowed in a single odds game, and stands to win $10 on the free-odds bet if the 7 is rolled before the 9 repeats, in addition to $10 on his don't pass bet. Should the point be rolled before the 7, the $15 free-odds bet and $10 don't pass bet will be lost.

If double odds were allowed, $20 would be the maximum allowable free-odds win. At 2 to 3 odds, the don't pass bettor would have to lay $30 to win $20.

Wrong Bettors Special Allowances — Single Odds Game

The casino makes a special provision for don't pass bettors when the point is a 5 or 9 and an odd figure such as $5 is wagered. Since the craps tables do not deal in half dollars, the player is allowed to make a free-odds bet of $9 behind the line in this instance, and if the bet is won, will get paid $6 ($9 at 2 to 3).

Whenever the point is 5 or 9 and the original bet is unequal, the house will allow the player to bet more than the straight single odds. Just ask the dealer the exact amount allowed in those instances for the rules vary from casino to casino.

Free-Odds: Come and Don't Come

Once a come point is established, the bettor can take odds (or lay odds for the don't come bet) and get the same advantageous payoffs, 2 to 1 on points 4 and 10 (1 to 2 for wrong bettors), 3 to 2 on the 5 and 9 (2 to 3), and 6 to 5 on the 6 and 8 (5 to 6).

The house has no advantage on these free-odds wagers, and like the line bets, the overall house edge on the come or don't come bets teamed with single odds drops to 0.8%, and with double odds, to 0.6%. The same special allowances apply for the come bets, in a single odds game; a three unit bet can be backed by five units if the point is 6 or 8, while a free-odds bet on points 5 and 9 can be backed by additional chips if the original come bet is uneven. In the double odds game, a two unit wager can be backed by five units if the point is a 6 or 8.

However, the odds bets on the come and don't come bets are placed differently than line bets. Rather than being made by the player, the odds bets are given to the dealer to place with the instruction, "odds on the come," or "odds on the don't come." The dealer will place the odds bet in the appropriate box atop the come point, but slightly offset, so that the odds bet can be differentiated from the come bet.

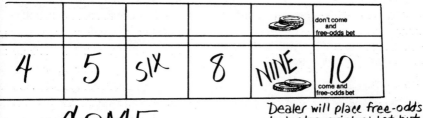

Dealer will place free-odds bet atop original bet but offset to distinguish from come or don't come bet.

The only other difference is with the come bet. While the come bet itself is working on the come-out roll, the odds bet on that come bet is not. Let's say the player had $15 bet on the come point of 6 and had that bet backed by $25 free-odds. A come-out roll of a 7 would of course be a loser for the $15 come bet, as that bet is always working, but since the free-odds bet was *off*, the $25 single odds wager would be returned to the player.

If a 6 was rolled instead, a winner for the come bet, the player would only win the $15, and be returned the $25 odds bet.

Though it is standard procedure for the free-odds bet backing the come wager to be off on the come-out roll, the player can request the odds bet to be on by informing the dealer that the "odds are on for the come bet," and then, of course, the odds bet is subject to the normal rules.

The odds on the don't come bets, as with the pass and don't pass wagers, are always working.

Let's look at some betting sequences to illustrate how the free-odds bets on come and don't come wagers work in conjunction with the line bets.

Right Bettors (Pass and Come Bets) -

Player A is a right bettor, he likes betting with the dice. His standard betting unit is $15 (3 units of $5) and this allows him to take advantage of the special free-odds allowances when the ponts are 5 and 9, and 6 and 8. Single Odds Game

Player Bets: $15 on the pass line.

The come-out roll is an 8, establishing 8 as the point.

Player Bets: $25 odds bet behind the 8 (5 unit special allowance bet).
$15 on the come.

The roll is a 4, establishing the 4 as a come point. Dealer moves Player A's bet from the come line to the box marked 4.

Player Bets: $15 odds bet on the 4. The dealer takes the wager and places it on the come bet but at a tilt to show it's an odds bet.
Player A decides to make another $15 come bet.

The roll is an 11. The new come bet is an automatic winner for $15. The other bets are unaffected.

Player Bets: $15 more on the come.

The roll is a 4, a winner on that come point. Player A wins $15 on the come bet and $30 (2 to 1 payoff) on the free-odds bet. The new $15 come bet is moved to the place box of 4, to indicate its come point.

Player Bets: $15 odds on the come point of 4.
$15 more on the come.
Player A now has a $15 pass line bet backed by $25 odds on the point of 8, a $15 come bet backed by $15 odds on the point of 4, and a new $15 come wager.

The roll is an 8, a winner on the pass line. Player A gets paid $15 on the pass line bet and $30 on his odds bet (6 to 5 odds) and these bets are removed from the layout. The new come bet is moved to the 8 box, the come point for that last bet. A new come-out roll will follow since the point was made.

Player Bets: $15 on the pass line.
$25 odds bet on his come point of 8.

The roll is a 7, a $15 winner on the new pass line bet, but a loser for the two come points of 4 and 8. Since the odds bets were off on the come-out roll, the $15 odds on the 4 and $25 odds on the 8 are returned to the player, leaving the player with only a $30 loss on the come points themselves, but a $15 winner on pass line bet.

Player A won $120 in bets and lost only $30 for a net win of $90.

Wrong Bettors (Don't Pass and Don't Come Bets)

Player B is a wrong bettor, he prefers to bet against the dice.

His standard betting unit is $20 because it's easier to figure the laying of odds with bets in multiples of $10.

Single Odds Game

Player Bets: $20 on the don't pass.

The come-out roll is a 6, establishing the 6 as a point.

Player Bets: $24 free-odds bet behind the 6 (laying 5 to 6 odds).
$20 on the don't come.

The roll is a 3, craps, a winner on the new don't come bet. The other bets are unaffected. The winning bet is removed from the layout.

Player Bets: $20 on the don't come again.

The roll is a 10, and the dealer moves the don't come bet above the box marked *10* to indicate the come point for the don't come bet.

Player Bets: $40 free-odds on the come point of 10 (laying 1 to 2 odds). The dealer takes the odds bet and places it atop the original bet but at a tilt so the bet can be distinguished from the don't come bet.
$20 bet on the don't come box.

The roll is a 9, establishing 9 as the come point for the new don't come bet. Player B now has bets against three points, the 4, 9 and 10. The roll of any of those point numbers is a loss for Player B on that particular number rolled, while the throw of a 7 will be a winner on all.

Player Bets: $30 free-odds on the 9, and decides not to make any more come bets.

The roll is a 6, a loser on the don't pass. Player B loses that $20 bet and the $24 odds bet behind it. Since the point was made, the next roll is a new come-out roll. All bets for the wrong bettor will be working.

Player Bets: $20 on the don't pass.

The roll is an 8, establishing 8 as the come point on the new don't pass bet.

Player Bets: $24 odds on the come point of 8, and decides not to make any further bets at this time.

The roll is a 7, a simultaneous winner on all the don't pass, don't come and odds bets. Player B wins $20 per wrong bet plus the $20 odds behind.

that bet for a $40 win per point. With three points covered, the total win on that 7 was $120.

Player B won $140 in bets and lost only $44 for a net win of $96.

B. The Rest of the Bets

With the exception of the place bets of 6 and 8, and Atlantic City Big 6 and Big 8, none of the bets presented in this section, which include the remainder of the bets possible at craps, are recommended for play. The house edge over the player on these bets is too large to be incorporated into a winning strategy, and the bettor making these bets will soon find himself drained of significant portions of his bankroll.

In fact, the majority of bets listed here are sucker bets, wagers that give the house an edge so exorbitant that the player stands no more than a slim chance of winning. Just because a bet is exotic looking and available doesn't mean that it should be bet on. To do well at craps, all bets with prohibitive odds must be avoided.

The bets listed in this section are discussed anyway so that the player has a full understanding of all the bets possible at craps, and so that the player is never tempted to make these poor wagers.

Place Bets

The place bets are among the most popular wagers in craps, and are a bet that a particular point number, whichever is wagered on, the 4, 5, 6, 8, 9, or 10, is rolled before a 7 is thrown. The player can make as many place bets as he wants, and some players do, covering all the numbers with place bets.

However, this is not recommended strategy, for as we will see, with the exception of the place bets of 6 and 8, the other place bets, the 4, 5, 9 and 10, are poor wagers, and will have no role in our winning strategies.

Place bets are made by giving the dealer the desired wager, and telling him, for example, to *place the 9*, or any such statement that indicates the player wants to make a place bet on the 9.

Though place bets can be made at any time, they are not working, or are **off** on the come-out roll, unless the player requests them to be **on** (working). The player can also request his place bets to be off for a limited series of throws, and may increase, reduce or remove them at any time prior to a roll.

The house payoffs on the place bets are as follows:

Bet	Payoff	Correct Odds	House Advantage
4 or 10	9 to 5	2 to 1	6.67%
5 or 9	7 to 5	3 to 2	4.00%
6 or 8	7 to 6	6 to 5	1.52%

To get the full payoffs on the place bets, the player should make his bets in the proper multiples. On place bets of 4 and 10, and 5 and 9, the bets should be made in multiples of $5 since the payoffs are 9 to 5 and 7 to 5 respectively. On the 6 and 8, the bet should be in multiples of $6 (7 to 6 payoff).

Excess bets in unequal multiples will be paid off at even-money only and work to the disadvantage of the player. For example, a $10 bet on the 6 will be paid as follows. The first $6 will get the full 7 to 6 odds for $7, while the remaining $4 gets paid at even-money, or $4, for a total win of $11. The last $4, paid off at only even-money, is a terrible payoff, and makes the entire bet a poor one.

Unless the player makes the place bets of 6 or 8 in multiples of $6 to insure full payoffs, the bet should not be make. Also, bets less than $5 on the 4, 5, 9 and 10, and less than $6 on the 6 and 8, will be paid off at only even-money.

To summarize, do not make place bets of 4 or 10, or 5 and 9, for the house edge is too high. The place bets of 6 and 8 have playable odds of 1.52 percent and can be used in an aggressive maximize gain strategy, though some players may prefer to stick with the line, come and don't come bets backed by free-odds, the best bets of all.

Big 6 and Big 8

The Big 6 and Big 8 are bets that a particular number bet on, the 6 or 8, is thrown before a 7 is rolled. These bets can be made at any time, and are bet by putting the wager into the box marked Big 6 or Big 8.

These bets work just like the place bets of 6 and 8 except that in Nevada casinos, the house only pays even-money on a won bet, while in Atlantic City, the bettor receives the same payoff he would receive had he made the place bets instead, 7 to 6.

Let's look at the correct odds. There are five ways to throw a winning 6 (or 8, if that is bet), and six ways to throw a losing 7, making the correct odds 6 to 5. The house pays only even-money on a won bet in Nevada, giving them a whopping 9.09% advantage. This makes the Big 6 and Big 8 terrible bets in Nevada, especially when they are compared to the 1.52% odds of the 6 and 8 place bets.

However, in Atlantic City, the Big 6 and Big 8 bets are paid off at 7 to 6 provided that the player bet in multiples of $6. This 7 to 6 payoff reduces the odds of the Big 6 and Big 8 to only 1.52%, just like the place bets of 6 and 8, and makes the Atlantic City Big 6 and Big 8 workable wagers for an aggressive maximize gain strategy.

Buying the 4 or 10

This is an option the casino gives the player when betting on a place number, and though it reduces the odds on the 4 or 10 from 6.67 percent to 4.76 percent, the buy bet is still a poor one and should not be made.

But here's how it works.

To *buy* the 4 or 10, you must give the house a 5 percent commission on your bet. Once you've bought a number, the house will pay off the bet at the correct odds. Thus, your payoff will be 2 to 1, the correct odds, rather than 9 to 5 as is usually the payoff for these place bets.

A five percent commission on $20 would be $1. For any bet smaller than $20, the commission would still be $1 since the craps tables generally carry no smaller units. In these cases, the house edge on your buy bet would be much larger than 4.76 percent. If you buy the 4 and 10 at $10 each, for a total of $20, the commission would only be 5 percent of the two bet total, or $1.

Like the place bets, buy bets are not working on the come-out roll, unless you instruct the dealer that the bet is *on*. They are also similar to the place bets in that they can be increased, reduced or removed at any time prior to the roll. Note that an increased buy bet is subject to the 5 percent commission on the additional wager.

Some casinos will keep the 5 percent commission if you decide to remove an established bet or charge an additional 5 percent if you win your bet and decide to let it ride.

Buying the 5, 6, 8, 9

Theoretically, you can buy these numbers as well, but since the commission is 5 percent, and the house edge on all these place bets is less than that, there is no advantage in buying these numbers.

Lay Bets

The lay bet is the opposite of a buy bet, and is used by wrong bettors who are wagering that the 7 will be thrown before the point or points they bet against is rolled. While the bet is paid off at correct odds, it costs the bettor 5 percent commission on the projected win to get this payoff, and is therefore, a poor bet.

Lay bets, which can be bet at any time, are made by giving the dealer your chips along with the required 5 percent commission on the projected win. The dealer will place the bet above the point number covered (in the area where the don't come bets are placed) and place a buy button on top to distinguish the lay bet.

To receive the full value on the lay bet of 4 or 10, the bettor would have to wager at least $40 to win $20 (1 to 2 odds). The 5 percent commission on the projected win of $20 would be $1. Any bet smaller than the $40 lay bet on the 4 or 10 would still be charged the mimimum $1 commission (craps tables do not generally deal in currency smaller than $1 chips) making the house edge greater than the 2.44% advantage already built into this wager.

The 5 and 9 lay bets would require a minimum wager of $30 for the player to get the maximum value. The potential $20 win (laying odds at 2 to 3) would be charged $1 commission. Again, a bet smaller than the projected win of $20 would still be charged the minimum $1 commission, and raise the overall house edge on the bet.

The 6 and 8 bets would require a wager of $24 at 5 to 6 odds on a projected win of $20 to get full value from the commission.

Points	House Advantage
4 or 10	2.44%
5 or 9	3.23%
6 or 8	4.00%

The lay bets can be added to, reduced or removed altogether at any time.

The player is advised not to make lay bets.

Field Bet

The field bet is a one roll wager that the next throw of the dice will be a number listed in the field box, the 2, 3, 4, 9, 10, 11 or 12. If one of the numbers not listed is rolled, the 5, 6, 7 or 8, then the bet is lost.

The field bet can be made at any time and is done by placing the wager in the area marked *Field*.

At first glance, the bet seems attractive. There are seven winning numbers listed in the field box, and two of these numbers, the 2 and the 12, pay double if they are rolled. In some casinos, the 2 or 12 pays triple. The other winning numbers, the 3, 4, 9, 10 and 11 pay even-money. But let's look closer.

The losing numbers, the 5, 6, 7 and 8, are the most frequently rolled numbers, and make up a total of 20 losing combinations. (Four ways to roll a 5, five ways to roll a 6, five ways to make an 8, and six ways to roll a 7 = 20). Adding up all the other numbers gives us a total of only 16 winning combinations. The 2 to 1 bonus on the 2 and the 12 is actually worth one more combination each for a total of 18 winning units, and where the 12 (or 2) is paid at 3 to 1, we get a total of 19 winners.

However, there are 20 combinations that will beat us, giving the house an edge of 5.55% when the 2 and 12 are paid at 2 to 1, and 2.7% when one is paid at 2 to 1 and the other at 3 to 1.

In either case, the house advantage is much larger than other bets available at craps, and the player should not make field bets.

Proposition, or Center Bets

The proposition, or center bets, as they are sometimes called, are located at the center of the layout, and are made by either giving the chips to the dealer who will pass them along to the stickman, or, as with the hardways bets or craps-eleven bet, can sometimes be tossed directly to the stickman.

The central area of the layout is under the complete domain of the stickman, and though he will physically handle the placing and removing of bets in this area, it is with the dealer that the player will generally make his bets and receive his payoffs.

The proposition bets are the worst bets a player can make at craps and should never be made. The house advantage ranges as high as 16.67 percent on some of these wagers. However, these bets are listed and their odds explained so that the reader will be fully conversant with all the wagers possible at craps.

Any Seven

This bet, which is that the following roll of the dice will be a 7, is paid off by the house at 4 to 1 (5 for 1), and is among the worst bets a player can make.

There are six ways to throw a 7 out of 36 possible combinations, making the odds one in six of throwing a 7 on any one roll, or equivalently, 5 to 1. Since the player is paid off at only 4 to 1, the house maintains an exorbitant edge of 16.67 percent over the player.

Don't even make this bet in your dreams.

Any Craps

This bet, located at the bottom of the center layout and along its sides, is a bet that the following roll will be a craps — a 2, 3 or 12.

There are four ways to roll a winner. The 2 and 12 account for one way each, while there are two ways to roll a three. The other 32 combinations are losers, making the correct odds 8 to 1. The house only pays 7 to 1, leaving them an 11.1 percent advantage.

2 or 12

This is a bet that the next roll of the dice will come up a 2, or a 12 if you bet that number, and is paid off by the house at 30 to 1.

Of the 36 possible combinations of the dice, there is only one way of rolling a 2 or a 12, making the correct odds 35 to 1 against rolling either number. With only a 30 to 1 payoff, the house enjoys a hefty 13.69 percent advantage.

Sometimes a casino may only pay off at 30 for 1, (29 to 1), giving them an edge of 16.67 percent. This should make no difference to us for we won't go near that bet in either case.

3 or 11

This is a wager that the following roll will be a 3, or an 11, whichever you place your money on, and the house payoff is 15 to 1.

Since there are only 2 ways to roll either number out of a possible 36 combinations, the correct odds are 17 to 1 (34 losers, 2 winners). The house edge is 11.1 percent. Where the payoff is 15 for 1 (14 to 1), this edge jumps to 16.67 percent.

Horn Bet

It takes four chips or multiples thereof to make this bet. The horn bet is a four way bet that the next roll will be a 2, 3, 11 or 12, in effect combining four poor bets together. The house pays off the winning number at the normal payoffs (15 to 1 for the 3 or 11, and 30 to 1 for the 2 or 12), and deducts the other three losing chips from the payoff.

This sucker bet combines four losing wagers for a combined house edge of 11.1 percent, or 16.67 percent with the poorer payoffs discussed earlier. Never make this bet.

Hop Bet

This one roll wager, which does not appear on the layout, is generally made on a combination of the dice not otherwise offered on the one roll bets such as 2, 3. If the bet is a pair such as 5, 5, the player will get the same payoff as the casino gives on the 2 or 12 bet (30 to 1 or 29 to 1). If the bet is a non-pair, such as 4, 5, which has two ways to win (4, 5; 5, 4), the payoff will be the same as on the 3, or 11 bet (15 to 1 or 14 to 1).

To make a hop bet, give your bet to the dealer or stickman, and call out for example "Hop 54," if the 5, 4 is the hop bet you wish to make.

With the more generous payoff hop bets give the casino an edge of 13.39%, otherwise the edge is 16.67%. In either case, consider the bet a donation to the casino. Never make these bets.

Craps-Eleven

The stickman will constantly exhort the player to make this horrendous bet, which is an appeal to bet the Any Craps and 11 bet simultaneously. We don't want to go near either bet by itself let alone together. Save your money for the show.

Hardways

Whenever the numbers 4, 6, 8 or 10 are rolled as doubles, the roll is said to be thrown **hardways**. A throw of 2, 2 is said to be 4, the hardway or hard 4, and similarly with 3, 3, 4, 4 and 5, 5 for hard 6, 8 and 10 respectively.

Rolling the 4, 6, 8 and 10 in other combinations is called **easy** such as 6, 4; 10 the easy way.

Betting hardways is betting that the particular number you choose comes up hard before it comes up easy or before a 7 is thrown.

Let's look at the odds involved.

Hard 4 and Hard 10

There is only one way to throw a hard 4 (2, 2) or hard 10 (5, 5), and eight ways to lose — six ways to roll a seven, and two ways to throw a 4 or 10 the easy way (1, 3, 3, 1; 6, 4, 4, 6).

The correct odds should be 8 to 1 but the house only pays 7 to 1 for an advantage of 11.1 percent. As with the other center bets, this bet is greatly disadvantageous to the player and should never be made.

Hard 6 and Hard 8

There are a total of 10 losing combinations — the 6 ways to roll a 7, and 4 ways to roll a 6 or an 8 the easy way. (There are a total of 5 ways to throw the 6 or 8, and subtracting the hardway, it leaves 4 other combinations). There is only 1 way to throw the 6 or 8 the hardway.

The correct odds of this hardway bet is 10 to 1 but the house only pays 9 to 1, giving them a commanding edge of 9.09 percent. Don't make this bet.

V. WINNING STRATEGIES

The underlying principle of all our winning strategies is to make only the best bets available, those with the lowest odds, for this gives us the best chances of winning. When used as we suggest, the overall house edge will be only 0.8 percent in a single odds game and 0.6 percent in a double odds one. We will never make any bet which gives the house an advantage greater than 1.52%, and in fact, the majority of our money will be placed on bets in which the house has no advantage whatsoever!

We'll play aggressively when winning, so that our winning sessions will be big, and when the dice go against us, we'll reduce our bets or even stop betting altogether. This will maximize our profits and minimize our losses, a smart money management technique that can put winnings in our pocket. And we'll follow the guidelines in the money management chapter, so that once we're winning big, we'll leave big winners.

This winning strategies chapter is divided into two main sections, one for right bettors, and the other for wrong bettors. The reader is reminded that betting right or wrong are equally valid approaches to winning, with equivalent odds, and that the choosing of either method is merely a matter of personal style.

Within each approach, right and wrong betting, we'll present the best strategies for the single and double odds game, and also the best methods for conservative and aggressive bettors to follow.

The Basic-Conservative methods presented are formulated for the cautious bettor, one who wants to get the best odds possible, but not risk substantial sums, while the Aggressive methods are more suited for the heavier bettor, one who is willing to risk more to win more. The two methods, Basic-Conservative and Aggressive, though, are equally powerful. The choice of one or the other depends solely on a player's bankroll considerations and financial temperament.

A. Winning Strategies: Betting with the Dice

In this section we're going to show how the right bettor, using sound principles of play can lower the house edge to the lowest possible figure, 0.8 percent in a single odds game and 0.6 percent in a double odds one. Using our methods, the majority of the right bettors wagers will be made on the free-odds bets, wagers that the house not only has no advantage whatsoever, but which if won, will pay the player more than he bet!

We'll use only the best bets in our basic strategies — the pass line, come and free-odds wagers, bets which give the player the best chances of winning. Built-in to the strategies are methods to turn winning sessions into big winning sessions without any risk of big losses. One of our maximizing profit strategies also employs the place bets of 6 and 8 (or Atlantic City Big 6 and Big 8), wagers that give the house a slightly higher edge, but which can be used to great advantage by an aggressive player during a hot roll.

Basic-Conservative Method - Right Bettors
Single Odds Strategy

Our standard bet will be in increments of three units so that we can take advantage of the special free-odds allowances should the points be 6 or 8, whereupon we can back our pass line or come bet by five units, or points 5 or 9, where we can bet extra if the original bet is uneven, such as $15, where $20 would be permitted as a free-odds wager.

This allows maximum usage of the free-odds bets, wagers the house has no edge on, and brings the overall house advantage down to the barest minimum possible in a single odds game.

These are the guidelines of our basic-conservative strategy:

1 — We will make three unit pass line and come bets until we have two points established, and back both those bets with the maximum single odds allowed.

2 — Every time a point repeats we will make another three unit pass line or come bet so that we continue to have two points working for us. If a 2, 3, 11, 12 declares a winner or a loser on the new pass line or come bet, we will follow with another bet until we get that second point established and then take the maximum single odds allowed on that point.

3 — If the shooter sevens-out, clearing the board of all bets, we'll begin the progression again with a new pass line bet.

Let's follow a sample shoot to see how the strategy works.

Player Bets: $15 (three $5 units) on the pass line.

The roll is a 9, establishing 9 as the point.

Player Bets: $20 (special allowance) single odds.
$15 come.

The roll is an 11, winner on the come. The winning bet is removed and the player makes another come bet.

Player Bets: $15 come.

The roll is a 6, establishing 6 as the come point.

Player Bets: $25 free-odds on the 6. Since the second point and free-odds bets have been established, no more bets are made.

The roll is a 9, winner on the pass line. The player wins $15 on the line bet and $30 on the odds for a total of $45. Only one point remains now, the come point on 6, so the player makes a pass line bet.

Player Bets: $15 on the pass line.

The roll is a 7, a $15 winner on the pass line, but a loser on the come point. Since the free-odds bets backing the come wagers are off on the come-out roll, the player loses only the $15 come bet and is returned the $25 odds bet.

The next bet should be a $15 pass line bet. The 7 cleared the layout of bets, some winning, some losing, and the new roll will be a come-out roll and the start of a new progression. The player won $75 and lost $15 for a total win of $60 in this short shoot.

Again, the Basic-Conservative bettor wants to have two points working for him at all times during a shoot, and will stop making additional bets once the two points are established, and single odds taken on each point.

Aggressive Method - Right Bettors

Rather than playing only two points as in the Basic-Conservative method, this strategy immediately attempts to establish three points. Otherwise, all the principles and methods are the same.

We begin by making a pass line bet. After a point is established, we will make a free-odds bet behind the pass line and a three unit come bet. When the come point is established, we will back that point with the maximum single odds allowed, and place yet another come bet backing that too with free-odds.

Once three points are established, we'll stop betting. Every time a point repeats and is paid off, we'll make another bet, so that at all times during a shoot we strive to have three points working for us. If the come point is made, we'll place another come bet. If it's the pass line, then we'll make another pass line bet. Like always, we'll back all our bets with the maximum single odds allowed.

If the shooter sevens-out, we'll start the sequence over again.

With three points covered, the bettor using this Aggressive method can make a lot of money when the shooter starts rolling numbers, especially when he utilizes our strategies for maximizing winning sessions.

Maximizing Profits - Methods For Right Bettors

The way to win big at craps is to play winning streaks aggressively so when points start repeating, our profits will mount quickly. The beauty of these strategies is that, while we give ourselves the opportunity of making huge profits, we never incur the risk of taking a devastating loss, for we'll only increase our bets when winning.

We won't start playing more aggressively until we're ahead by at least 20 units as Basic-Conservative players and 25 units as Aggressive players. For $1 bettors making standard bets of $3, that means $20 and $25 respectively, for $5 bettors making standard bets of $15, that means $100 and $125, while for $25 chip players betting $75 a play, it means $500 and $625 respectively.

Theoretically, we could increase our bet size before this time, but that leaves our bankroll vulnerable to bad runs of luck. The concept is to play aggressively on their money, not ours.

We wait until all our points are established and working before increasing our bets.

Let's say we're betting $15 as our basic three unit bet ($5 units), and have already established the pass line point with single odds on the 8, and two come points with single odds on the 5 and 10. We now have three points working for us, the basic plan for the Aggressive Method, and see that we're already ahead 27 units.

Our strategy now works as follows. Every time a point repeats and we get paid off, instead of re-establishing an additional come or pass line point at the basic three unit bet, we increase that bet by three units to six units, and back the new bet with maximum single odds. Thus, on a six unit bet, points 4 and 10 can be backed by six units, 5 and 9 by six units,* and 6 and 8 by ten units.

Let's say points 8 and 10 have repeated and we have made six unit bets on the new pass and come wagers. The new points thrown are 9 on the come bet and a 10 on the pass line. So as it stands, we have six unit bets on the 9 and 10 (both bets backed by the full odds) and three units on the come point of 5. Should the 10, our pass line point repeat, our new bet would be six units, for our other point, the 5, still has only a three unit bet on it. Do not increase bets to higher levels (in this example, above 6 units) until all the points have been brought up to the same bet size.

---

* If the bet is uneven on points 5 and 9, more than six units can be bet as a free-odds wager, but if the bet is even and can be paid at 3 to 2, the special allowance wouldn't apply.

If the streak continues and all the basic pass and come bets have been brought up to six unit bets, begin to reestablish won points by making pass and come bets in units of nine, and of course, backing all these bets with the maximum single odds allowed. Increase bets in this fashion for as long as the streak continues.

This steady progressive increase of bets allows us to maximize the profits resulting from a hot roll while protecting us against a sudden seven-out making serious inroads into our winnings.

As an alternate and more aggressive way of increasing won bets, the bettor could increase each won bet by three units regardless of how many units were already placed on the other points. Thus, a bet that repeated twice in a row, could have a nine unit bet on it while the other points were covered by only three units each.

We make our bet increases in units of three so that we can continue to take advantage of the special three unit single odds allowances.

DO NOT begin new progressions (after a shooter sevens-out) at a level higher than three units. This is very important. A bettor that continues to bet in amounts higher than his initial standard three unit wager is susceptible to a short losing streak wiping out his hard earned gains in a matter of a few bad shoots. We will only bet more aggressively during a hot streak, and will not try to anticipate one occurring.

Once we've had our one great shoot we'll never give the casino a chance to get our winnings back. We'll return to our basic three unit bet. If things go poorly, we'll call it quits soon afterwards, a huge winner. If the shooter gets hot again, we'll start increasing our bets and winnings, always ready for the next big kill.

This is smart money management, the key to success for winners.

Very Aggressive Method For Maximizing Profits
Place Bets of 6 and 8 and Atlantic City Big 6 and Big 8

The main advantage of this hard-hitting strategy is that it allows the bettor to cover the most frequently rolled points, the 6 and 8, during every hot shoot, with a chance to make enormous profits should that hot shoot continue. But to do this requires that the bettor risk larger sums of money,* and that he gives the house a slightly higher edge of 1.52 percent on one or two bets during each betting cycle.

For this reason, many right bettors may prefer to stay with the pass and come bets backed by the maximum free-odds to have the best odds possible at all times, and to use either the strategy for increasing individual bets, or the establishing of additional points through pass and come bets as their method for maximizing profits during a hot roll.

To achieve the best results and minimize the risks involved in using this very aggressive betting approach, we'll follow two rules. First, we'll never make place bets of 6 and 8 (or Atlantic City Big 6 and Big 8) until all our desired points have been established through pass and come bets (according to the dictates of our strategies), and will then only place bet the 6 and 8 if these points are not already covered by one of our line or come bets. The place bets of 6 and 8 and Atlantic City Big 6 and Big 8 should never be made in place of our basic line bets (backed by free-odds), for we don't want to replace bets of 0.6 or 0.8 percent odds with bets giving the house an edge of 1.52 percent.

Second, we will employ this strategy only when winning. We don't want to risk accumulation of heavy losses if we're already in the hole, but at the same time, we allow ourselves the opportunity to win big without risking a bad loss.

Following these two rules gives us the best of both worlds. We not only get the good odds on our pass and come bets backed by the maximum free-odds, but can also cover the 6 and 8, the heart of all hot shoots, if they are not already covered.

Though more effective when used in conjunction with the Aggressive Strategy (3 points covered), place bets could also be made with the Basic-Conservative Strategy according to the same principles. The strategy also works equally well with the single or double odds game. Here's how the strategy works.

Once three points are established and working for the right bettor in a single or double odds game, he should make place bets on 6 and 8 (or Big 6 and Big 8 in Atlantic City) if those point numbers are not already covered by the pass and come bets.

Example: The come out roll establishes the 6 as the point, and the following two rolls establish the 4 and 5 as come points. The Aggressive Strategy player now has three points covered and

---

* This, of course, is in accordance with the old gambling truth — To win more, you have to risk more. Money management concerns should be foremost in the decision to bet this aggressively.

backed by the maximum free-odds allowed. Since the 8 is not covered as a point and will be one of the central numbers if the dice get hot, a place bet on 8 should be made.

Every time a 6 or 8 is repeated, the player should make an additional place bet to re-establish the point. If another point is made, say the come point of 4, another bet should be wagered, for we always want three pass and come bets working during each shoot. Should the following roll establish a 6 as the come point, the place bet on 6 should be taken down, for we would rather have the point covered with the lower odds of the line and free-odds bet.

Sometimes only three points will be covered using this method, the 6, 8 and one other, while other times, as many as five points will be covered. For instance, if the first three points covered on the pass and come points are 4, 9 and 10, we would make place bets of 6 and 8, for during a shoot, we always want to cover these frequently rolled points.

Keep the level of the place bets of 6 and 8 similar to the level used on your other bets and remember to make these bets in multiples of six so that we can get the full 7 to 6 payoff. And during hot rolls, we'll follow our procedures for increasing the standard pass and come bets, remembering to return to the standard bet size once our run is over.

Double Odds Strategies

Whenever the bettor has a choice, he should always choose a double odds game over a single odds game, for the additional allowance of the free-odds bets drops the overall house edge from 0.8 percent to 0.6 percent when using our methods.

The playing strategies we will pursue in the double odds game are identical to the single odds game except that we will bet in units of two instead of units of three as recommended in the single odds game to take advantage of the special five unit free-odds allowance when the point is 6 or 8. Basic-Conservative bettors should establish two points with maximum double odds on each, while Aggressive bettors will want to cover three points.

Follow the procedures for the single odds methods substituting only the two unit basic bet for the three unit bets, and making double odds bets instead of single odds.

Maximizing Profits — Double Odds Game

Again our strategy here will follow that of the single odds game except we'll be increasing our bets by two units instead of three.

Basic-Conservative bettors will not begin increasing bets until they've accumulated 20 units in profits, and Aggressive bettors will need 25 units.

Remember to take advantage of the special allowances when the point is a 6 or 8. A four unit bet can be backed by 10 units in the double odds game, and a six unit bet by 15.

When eventually the shooter sevens-out, ending our winning streak, we'll start the next progression again at two units, ready to capitalize on another hot roll should one develop.

B. Winning Strategies: Betting Against the Dice

Though the odds of winning are equivalent to the right betting strategies, 0.8 percent in a single odds game and 0.6 percent in a double odds game, very few craps players bet against the dice. Many bettors feel uncomfortable about having to lay odds, putting more money on their free-odds bet than they will win should the bet be won, but as stated earlier, the free-odds wagers give the house no edge betting right or wrong.

However, players that bet wrong don't mind giving the odds, for the roll of a 7, their winner, will occur more often than any point number, and they'll have frequent winners. In addition, should a point be repeated, a losing roll for wrong bettors, only one bet will be lost. The other points covered by the wrong bettor are still in play. On the other side of the dice, the right bettors fear the 7, for when it is thrown, all their established points and free-odds bets are lost.

We will apply the same principles of play as right bettors. We'll make only the best bets available to us, those that reduce the house edge to the lowest possible figure — the don't pass, the don't come and free-odds bets.

Basic Conservative Method — Wrong Bettors
Single Odds Strategy

Our standard bet will be in even increments of two units. Bets such as $15 or $25 are difficult to work with when the point is a 5 or 9 and 2 to 3 odds should be laid. Betting in other unit sizes is equally valid, but the player will find it easiest to work in multiples of $10.

These are the guidelines of our Basic-Conservative strategy:

1 —We will make two unit don't pass and don't come bets until we have established bets against two points, and back both those bets with maximum free-odds.

2 —Should a point repeat, a loser for us, we will make another don't come or don't pass bet, so that we can continue to have bets working against two points. If a 2, 3, 11 or 12 determines a winner or loser on a new don't pass or don't come bet, we will follow with another bet until we get that second point established, and then we'll lay the maximum single odds against that point.

3 — Stop establishing don't pass and don't come bets if a second point repeats. This is an important safeguard to protect us against bad losing streaks.

4 —If a 7 is thrown, a winner on all our bets, we'll begin the progression again with our two unit don't pass bet.

5 —Follow the recommendations in the Maximizing Profits section for advice on how to increase winnings when the dice are going our way.

As cautious bettors, we'll limit ourselves to a coverage of only two points and strictly follow the safeguard recommended in step three.

Here's a sample shoot to illustrate the strategy.

Player Bets: $20 on don't pass.

The come-out roll is an 8, establishing 8 as the point.

Player Bets: $24 single odds (laying 5 to 6 odds).
         $20 don't come.

The roll is a 3, a $20 winner on the new don't come bet. Another don't come bet is made to get a second point established.

Player Bets: $20 don't come.

The roll is an 8, a $20 loser on the don't pass bet and $24 loser on the free-odds bet. The new don't come bet now has 8 as its come point. Since only one point is ocvered, another don't pass bet is made. The next roll is a come-out roll. Should the shooter get hot and make an additional point, we'll employ our safeguards and stop making additional bets.

Player Bets: $24 odds on the come point of 8.
         $20 don't pass.

The come-out roll is a 4, establishing 4 as the point.

Player Bets: $40 odds on the don't pass point of 4 (laying 1 to 2).

The roll is a 6, a neutral throw on this shoot.

Player Bets: No more bets. Two points are established, and free-odds have been taken on both bets.

The roll is a 7, winner on both points and free-odds bets, for a total win of $80 on that throw.

The player has won $100 and lost $46 for a win of $54 on this short shoot. The progression starts again with a $20 don't pass bet.

Aggressive Method — Wrong Bettors

Our Aggressive strategy follows the same guidelines as the Basic-Conservative method except that we will cover three points during a shoot instead of two, and will stop making additional don't pass and don't come bets if three points repeat, instead of two as advised in the Basic-Conservative method. We'll use the same bets — the don't pass, don't come and free-odds bets, and enjoy the same low 0.8 percent house edge in a single odds game.

We begin by making a don't pass bet, and backing that with the maximum single odds once the point is established. Then, we'll make two successive don't come wagers, or as many as necessary, until two points are established, and will back those bets with maximum single odds as well. Once we have bets established against three points, we'll stop betting.

Should a 2, 3, 11 or 12 be rolled before all the points are established, we'll make another don't come bet until that third point is set. And we'll strictly adhere to our safeguard. If a third point repeats, we'll stop making additional bets during the cycle, and just ride out the unlucky streak. We never want to bet into a losing streak.

When the shooter sevens-out, a winner on all our bets, we'll start our cycle again, establishing three points with the maximum single odds.

Maximizing Profits — Methods for Wrong Bettors

The safest and most effective way of winning big at craps is to increase bets only during cold runs,* when the dice are going our way. The concept is to parlay winnings into big winnings. We do this by increasing bets only after a winning cycle, when the dice have already declared themselves, and never after a losing bet. Players and systems that attempt to regain lost money by increasing their bets only court disaster, for this type of desperate betting leaves one vulnerable to huge losses, and that's bad money management.

We won't start playing more aggressively until we're ahead by at least 20 units as a Basic-Conservative player and 25 units as an Aggressive method player. This gives us the opportunity to make big profits when the dice are with us, while protecting us against ever getting hurt by a bad run. And as a matter of fact, if the basic wrong betting safeguards and the stop-loss advice in the money

---

* "Cold" runs favor the wrong bettor.

management section are adhered to, we'll never take a crippling loss. But we're always ready to win big.

Unlike the right bettors strategies where bets are increased during a cycle, we will wait until the shooter sevens-out, a winner for us, before we begin to play more aggressively. Once you're ahead the aforementioned amounts, and the previous betting cycle was a winning one, increase the basic bet by two units.

If all our points were covered by two unit basic bets, we'll now cover the points by four unit basic bets, and if after the shooter sevens-out, we have emerged winners again, we'll continue to bet into the winning streak, and up our bet by another two units, to six units. We'll continue to increase bets by two units as long as the streak continues, all the time backing the bets with the maximum single odds allowed.

If the basic bet was $10 (two units of $5), the next basic bet will be $20, and then $30 and so on.

Anytime a sequence has been a losing one, begin the following shoot at the original two unit basic bet. In the example above, we would begin again at $10. Smart money management dictates that we only increase bets during a winning streak.

All the time during a shoot, we'll follow the safeguards outlined in the strategies. Basic-Conservative method bettors will stop establishing points should two points be repeated, and Aggressive method bettors will hold their bets if a third point repeats.

Let's follow a progression to see how this works.

We'll assume the player is betting $10 as a standard bet and had just won a sequence when the shooter sevened-out. The bettor is following the Basic-Conservative method, covering two points. He's now ahead 21 units ($5 units), and ups the basic bet to $20 (four units).

Player Bets: $20 don't pass.
The come-out roll is a 4, establishing 4 as the point.

Player Bets: $40 single odds on the 4 (laying 1 to 2).
$20 don't come.
The roll is an 8, establishing 8 as the come point.

Player Bets: $24 single odds against the 8 (laying 5 to 6), and makes no more don't come or don't pass bets since his two points are already established with maximum single odds,
The next roll is a 9, no effect on the established bets.
The next roll is a 7, $40 total winner on the don't come and don't pass

bets, and $40 win on the odds bets, for a total win of $80 on this sequence.

The player is still doing well, being ahead a total of 37 units, and ups the basic bet two units more, to $30.

Player Bets: $30 don't pass.

The come-out roll is a 5, establishing 5 as the point.

Player Bets: $45 single odds on the 5 (laying 2 to 3).
$30 don't come.

The roll is a 2, $30 winner on the new don't come bet.

Player Bets: $30 on the don't come, trying to establish that second point.

The roll is a 10, establishing 10 as the come point.

Player Bets: $60 single odds on the 10. Both points are fully established now.

The roll is a 5, $75 loser on that point ($30 don't pass and $45 free-odds).

Player Bets: $30 on the don't pass. If another point repeats, the player will stop establishing points, safeguarding himself against a bad loss.

The roll is a 7, a $30 loser on the new don't pass bet, but a $60 winner on the 10 ($30 don't come, $30 free-odds), for a total of $90 in wins and $105 in losses. Since this progression was a loser, the player starts the following sequence at the basic $10 two unit bet, protecting his current winnings of 34 units ($170).

Players using the Aggressive method and covering three points instead of the two illustrated in the above example, will apply the same principles — increasing bets when winning, and reverting to the original basic bet if a betting cycle is lost.

Double Odds Strategy — Wrong Bettors

Whenever possible, the wrong bettor should play a double odds game over a single odds game for it lowers the overall house edge from 0.8 to 0.6 percent. The major drawback to the double odds game is that the bettor must lay out a lot more money than the single odds game due to the nature of wrong betting, so we compensate by playing no more than two points.

This strategy is identical to the Basic-Conservative single odds method, except that we're laying double odds instead of single odds. We'll begin by making a don't pass bet, and backing that bet by double odds once the point is established. If $10 is the line bet, $40 will be the double odds bet if the point is 4 or 10, $30 if the point is 5 or 9, and $24 if the point is 6 or 8. Then we make a don't come bet and lay double odds on the come point.

We attempt to keep two points working for us and no more. If a point repeats, we'll make another don't come or don't pass bet to re-establish the point, backing it with double odds, but should a second point repeat, we'll wait until the shooter sevens-out before we make any additional don't pass or don't come bets.

Double Odds Strategy — Maximizing Gains

It is recommended that the bettor increase his wagers cautiously when playing a double odds game. The mushrooming effect of double odds can rapidly increase the outlay of money on the table, so we want to be conservative in our increases. For example, a $10 bettor may want to increase bets by only $5, since each $5 increase could call for an additional double odds bet of $20 if the point were a 4 or 10. Use your own discretion for bet increases, possibly one unit per winning cycle.

We'll use the same principles outlined in the single odds Basic-Conservative strategy for increasing bets. We'll increase only during a winning streak and not before we're up at least 20 units.

VI. Money Management

The speed with which money can change hands at craps makes intelligent use of one's monetary resources a vital part of the winning formula. Extreme fluctuations are normal in gambling, and the ability to successfully deal with these pendulous swings of fortune often separates the winners from the losers.

To be a winner, a player must have emotional control, for the temptation to ride a winning steak too hard in hopes of a big killing or to bet wildly during a losing streak, trying for a quick comeback, are two of the most common factors that destroy a large number of gamblers. Inevitably, the big winning sessions quickly dissipate into small wins or even disastrous losses, while moderately bad losing sessions can turn into a nightmare.

Smart money management also necessitates that the player have a bankroll sufficiently large enough to withstand the normal fluctuations common to craps. Undercapitalization (or over-betting) leaves a player vulnerable in two ways. First, a limited money supply can be devastated by a normal downward trend. Second, and quite common, the bettor may feel pressured by his shortage of funds and play less powerfully than smart strategy dictates.

This leads to the cardinal rule in all gambling, and a point that must be thoroughly understood before you ever go near any gaming table.

NEVER GAMBLE WITH MONEY YOU CANNOT AFFORD TO LOSE EITHER FINANCIALLY OR EMOTIONALLY. The importance of this rule cannot be overemphasized. A player that gambles with needed funds, gambles foolishly, for gambling involves chance, and the short run possibilities of a player taking a loss are real, no matter how good the odds may be.

Gambling should be viewed as a form of entertainment, both monetarily and emotionally. If you cannot afford the possibility of losing your gambling bankroll, either bet at a lower affordable level, or don't play at all. Players that disregard this rule are no longer playing for fun, and are starting to play compulsively. And playing with what is referred to as "scared money" is a certain way for these gamblers to guarantee themselves painful losses.

The emotional level is just as important. Once the playing of the game becomes a cause for anxiety, for whatever reason, and ceases to become a form of entertainment, then it is time to take a breather. You won't play as well because your mind will be preoccupied by the possibility of losing and perhaps more importantly, you will receive no emotional satisfaction from the game.

The goal is not only to win at craps, but to make the experience of playing as pleasurable as possible. This means that you should never gamble if you're emotionally unprepared to risk money, do not feel confident or alert, or any other factor that will adversely affect your playing.

Play again later on, when you feel more alert and confident, and you will have the necessary ingredients of a winner — emotional control. Remember the casinos aren't going anywhere.

Money management skills can be categorized as follows:

a. Bankrolling (Total bankroll, table bankroll).

b. When to Quit (Maximize profits, minimize losses).

Read this section carefully, for these money management skills will not only protect you from ever losing more than you can afford to, but when combined with our powerful playing strategies, will give you the best chances of winning at craps.

Bankrolling

The amount of money necessary to withstand the normal fluctuations common to craps will vary according to the type of strategy you employ (right or wrong betting), the aggressiveness of your approach (Basic-Conservative or Aggressive), and your expected playing time.

We'll discuss the single session bankroll first for the various strategies, and then present the type of bankroll the player will need for longer sessions at the craps table.

Single Session Bankroll

a. Right Bettors

Chart 8
Single Session Bankroll: Right Bettors

Approach (Points Covered)	Units Needed for a Single Cycle	Table Bankroll Needed
Basic-Conservative (2 points)	14	100
Aggressive (3 points)	21	150

Above figures apply to both single and double odds games.

1. Basic-Conservative Strategy

In the single odds game, Basic-Conservative bettors will cover two points through pass and come bets and back both points with the maximum single odds allowed. Since the standard line bet will be three units, and the single odds bet backing the pass and come will be between three to five units, we can expect each point to require a total of six to eight units to be fully covered, or about 14 units to fully cover each cycle of two points.

In the double odds game, our standard line bet of two units will be backed with the maximum double odds allowed, or about four to five units for a total of six to seven units per point. Fully covering a cycle of two points will require about 14 units, the same as the single odds game.

2. Aggressive Strategy

Aggressive strategy bettors will need roughly 21 units to fully cover their three points in a single or double odds game.

To play safe, and give himself sufficient funds, the bettor should have enough of a table stake for about seven betting cycles. The above chart sums up these requirements.

b. Wrong Bettors

Chart 9
Single Session Bankroll: Wrong Bettors

Approach (Points Covered)	Units Needed for a Single Cycle	Table Bankroll Needed
Basic-Cons. — Single Odds (2)	12	85
Basic-Cons. — Double Odds (2)	20	150
Aggressive — Single Odds (3)	18	125
Aggressive — Double Odds (3)	We recommend against covering three points with the maximum double odds.	

1. Basic Conservative Strategy

In the single odds game, our basic betting size will be two units,* and we'll cover two points. We'll back each point by four units, the maximum single odds allowed, for a total of six units bet on each point, or a total of 12 units to cover a full cycle of two points.

The nature of double odds betting for the wrong bettor requires a larger initial outlay of funds than for the right bettors, and hence, a larger single session bankroll is needed. We'll back each two units standard bet by eight units, the maximum double odds allowed, for a total of 10 units needed to fully cover each point, or 20 units for a cycle of two points.

2. Aggressive Strategy

Aggressive Strategy bettors will need about 18 units to cover a full cycle of three points in a single odds game, and as mentioned earlier in the Winning Strategy section, we won't cover three points in a double odds game as wrong bettors.

As with the right bettors, the player should have a table bankroll for seven betting cycles. The above chart sums up these requirements.

Total Bankroll

The longer one plans on playing craps, the larger one's bankroll must be to cover the inevitable fluctuations. The following bankroll requirements have been formulated to give the player enough capital to survive any reasonable losing streak, and be able to bounce back on top.

---

* For players that bet in unit sizes other than two units, they can figure the table stake needed by estimating the number of units needed for one full cycle of play, and multiplying that number by seven.

Chart 10
Total Bankroll Requirements: Right Bettors

Approach (Points Covered)	Single Session Stake	One Day Bankroll	Weekend Bankroll
Basic-Conservative (2 points)	100	500	700
Aggressive (3 points)	150	750	1000

Above figures apply to both single and double odds games.

Chart 11

Approach (Points Covered)	Single Session Stake	One Day Bankroll	Weekend Bankroll
Basic-Conservative (2 points)			
Single Odds Game	85	425	600
Double Odds Game	150	750	1000
Aggressive (3 points)			
Single Odds Game	125	625	875
Double Odds Game	We recommend against covering three points with the maximum double odds.		

The bankroll needed for a full day's session should be about five times that of a single session, and the weekend's bankroll should be about seven times that of a single sesison. Players that plan on gambling for considerably longer durations will need about ten times a single session's stake.

However, we advise against the player overdoing it at the craps tables, for though we have reduced the house edge to the lowest possible amount, and give the player the best chances of winning, that small house edge can grind out the bettor over extended sessions of play.

The unit size chosen by the player will depend upon the level of betting he prefers. A high roller accustomed to making large wagers may bet $75 a play (three units of $25 chips), and would need 100 units of $25 or $2500, for a table session using the right bettors Basic-Conservative strategy. On the other hand, a $3 bettor (three units of $1) playing the same strategy would multiply the unit size, $1, by 100, and would need $100 to play a single session at the $3 standard bet level.

This does not mean the player must have all the money out on the table when playing, but that that money should be readily available in his pocket in case it's needed. And as you will see later in the minimizing losses section, we will never use all our table stake in any one sesion but will restrict our losses should luck go against us. This way we'll never get hurt by an unlucky session.

If you arrive at the casinos with a definite amount of money to gamble with, and want to figure out how much your unit size bet should be, simply take your gambling stake and divide it by the amount of units you need to have for the particular strategy you want to play. If you bring $500 with you and were to spend a day using the right bettors Basic-Conservative strategy, you would divide $500 by the 500 units (Total Bankroll column). Your basic unit should be $1, and since right bettors will be betting in units of three, the standard pass or come bet would be $3. If you were to play the Aggressive strategy, 750 units would be needed for a days bankroll.

When to Quit

What often separates the winners from the losers is — the winners, when winning, leave the table a winner, and when losing, restrict their losses to affordable amounts. Smart gamblers never allow themselves to get destroyed at the table.

As a player, you have one big advantage that, if properly used, will assure you success as a gambler — you can quit playing whenever you want to. To come out ahead, you must minimize your losses when you lose and maximize your gains when you win. This way, your winning session will eclipse your losing sessions and you will come out an overall winner.

Our winning strategies for both the right and wrong bettors, Basic-Conservative or Aggressive style, are carefully formulated to not only give the player the best odds possible to receive at craps, but also to allow this minimize loss, maximize gain principle to work to our advantage.

We will stick by the principle stressed throughout the winning strategies section — When losing, we will reduce our bets or stop betting altogether, and when winning, and only when winning, we will increase our bets to maximize profits during winning streaks.

Minimizing Losses

Here are some simple guidelines that, if followed, will save you a lot of money.

1 —Right bettors: Limit your table losses to 70 units for Basic-Conservative bettors, and 100 units for Aggressive bettors. If betting $5 chips ($15 standard line bet), never lose more than $350 and $500 respectively in any one session; if $1 chips ($3 standard line bet), then $70 for Basic Conservative bettors and $100 for Aggressive bettors.

Wrong bettors: Wrong bettors should limit their table losses to the same levels as right bettors in a single odds game, but in a double odds game, loss limits should be 100 units for the Basic-Conservative players and 150 units for the Aggressive players.

Do not dig in for more money, and you can never be a big loser. Take a break, try again later. You never want to get into a position where losing so much in one session totally demoralizes you.

2 —Never increase your bet range beyond your bankroll capabilities. In other words, always bet within your means.

3 —Never increase your bet size to catch up and break even. Raising it will not change the odds of the game, nor will it change your luck. What it will do is make your chances of taking a terrible beating frighteningly high. As before, do not get into a position where losing so much in one session destroys any reasonable chance of coming out even. You can't win all the time. Rest a while, you'll get them later.

Protecting Your Wins

Once winning, the most important thing in craps is to walk away a winner. There is nothing worse than leaving the table a loser after having been up a lot of money. Once your wins at a table have exceeded half to two-thirds your table stake (or less if you desire), you should put aside a substantial portion of those funds into a "don't touch" pile, and play with the rest of the winnings. If a losing streak ensues and you lose that winning buffer, you have protected yourself. You walk away with winnings in your pocket.

Let's say you're playing the Basic-Conservative strategy and are in the middle of a hot run. You see that you're ahead 80 units. Put away 40 of those units, and play with the other 40. As long as the hot run continues, you will continually put winnings aside into the "don't touch" pile, and of course, according to our maximize gains strategies, we'll increase bets. However, once that streak ends, and our buffer seems to be wearing away, quit, and you'll quit a big winner.

VIII. GLOSSARY

Advantage, Casino Advantage — The built-in odds that favor the casino over the player. Also known as **Edge** or **House Edge**.

Any Craps — A bet that the following roll will be a 2, 3, or 12.

Any Seven — A bet that the following roll will be a 7.

Back Line — Refers to the don't pass area.

Bar the 12 — A term found in the don't pass and don't come areas which makes the roll of a 12 (in some casinos the 2) a standoff between the wrong player and the house.

Big 6, and Big 8 — A bet that the 6, or the 8, whichever is bet on, will be thrown before a 7 is rolled.

Black Chips — $100 chips.

Boxman — Casino executive who supervises the craps table from a seat located between the two standing dealers.

Box Numbers — The boxes numbered 4, 5, 6, 8, 9 and 10, which are used to mark the point, and to mark place, come and buy bets.

Buy Bets — Instead of place betting a number, a player option to buy a point number, and get paid at the correct odds. However, a 5% commission must be paid to buy the number.

Call Bet — A verbal bet that a wager is working. Disallowed in many casinos by the indication "No Call Bets" on the layout.

Center Bets — see Proposition Bets.

Color Change — The changing of chips to a higher or lower denomination.

Cold Dice — A streak of losing rolls for the right bettors. Good for wrong bettors.

Come Bet — A bet that the dice will win, or pass. Works just like a pass bet except that it can only be made after a point is established.

Come-Out Roll — The roll made before any point has been established.

Coming Out — A term to designate that a new come-out roll is about to happen.

Correct Odds — The mathematical likelihood that a bet will be a winner, expressed in odds.

Crap Out — The roll of a 2, 3, or 12 on a come-out roll, an automatic loser for pass line bettors.

Craps — Term used to denote a 2, 3 or 12. Also the name of the game.

Craps-Eleven — A one roll bet combining the Any Craps and 11.

Cycle — The term designating the establishing of all bets in a betting strategy.

Dealer — The casino employee who works directly with the player and who handles all monetary transactions and bets.

Dice — The two six-sided cubes, numbered one to six, that are used to play craps.

Don't Come Bet — A bet made against the dice. The bet works just like the don't pass except that it can only be made after a point is established.

Don't Pass — A bet made before a point is established, on the come-out roll only, that the dice will lose.

Double Odds Bet — A free-odds bet that allows the player to bet double his line wager as a right bettor, and double the line payoff as a wrong bettor.

Easy, Easy Way — The throw of a 4, 6, 8, or 10 other than as a pair, such as 1:5, 6 the easy way.

Edge, House Edge — see **Advantage**, **Casino Advantage**.

Even-Money — The payoff of one dollar for every dollar bet.

Field Bet — A one-roll bet that the next roll of the dice will be a number in the field box — a 2, 3, 4, 9, 10, 11 or 12.

Floorman — Casino executive who supervises one or more craps tables.

Free-Odds Bets — A bet made in conjunction with the line, come and don't come bets, that can only be made after the establishment of a point for that bet. The free-odds bet is paid off at the correct odds and the house has no advantage on these wagers.

Front Line — Refers to the pass line.

Hardway Bet — A sequence bet that the hardway number, the 4, 6, 8 or 10 will come up in doubles before it comes up easy, or before a 7 is thrown.

Hardway — The throw of a 4, 6, 8 or 10 as a pair, such as 3, 3; 6 the hardway.

Hop Bet — A bet that the next throw of the dice will be a specific number combination usually not found on the layout.

Horn Bet — A one roll bet that the next throw will be a 2, 3, 11 or 12.

Hot Roll — An extended succession of winning throws for players betting with the dice. Bad for wrong bettors.

House — A term to denote the Casino.

Inside Numbers — The place numbers 5, 6, 8 and 9.

Lay Bet — A wager made by wrong bettors that a 7 will show before the point number wagered on is thrown.

Layout — The felted surface of the craps table where all bets are placed, paid off and collected, and where the dice are thrown.

Line Bet — Refers to a pass or don't pass bet.

Marker — An IOU signed by a player with established credit at a casino.

Marker Buck — Round disk used to mark either the point or to indicate that no point is yet established. Also called **Puck**, or **Marker Puck**.

Nickels — $5 chips, usually red in color.

Odds Bet — See **Free-Odds Bet**.

Off — A designation that a bet is not working on a particular roll.

On — A designation that a bet is working on a particular roll.

One Roll Bet — A bet whose outcome is determined on the very next throw of the dice.

Outside Numbers — The place numbers 4, 5, 9 and 10.

Parlay or Press — The increase of a won bet, usually by doubling it.

Pass, Pass Line — A bet made before a point is established, on the come-out roll only, that the dice will pass, or win.

Payoff, House Payoff — The amount of money the casino pays the player on a winning bet.

Pit Boss — Supervisor of the gaming tables.

Place Bet — A wager that a particular box number, whichever is bet on, the 4, 5, 6, 8, 9 or 10, will be rolled before a 7.

Point, Point Number — The throw of a 4, 5, 6, 8, 9 or 10 on the come-out roll becomes the point number.

Proposition or **Center Bets** — The bets located in the center of the layout.

Quarters — $25 chips, usually green in color.

Right Bettors — Players betting that the dice will pass. Pass and come bettors.

Roll or Throw — An individual toss of the dice.

Sequence Bet — A bet whose outcome is not necessarily determined on the following roll but may take a succession of rolls to be determined.

Seven-Out — The roll of a 7 after a point has been established, a loser for pass line bettors.

Shoot — A progression of rolls ending on either an immediate decision on the come-out roll, or the sevening-out after a point had been established.

Shooter — The player throwing the dice.

Silver — $1 tokens or dollar chips.

Single Odds — A free-odds bet that allows the player to bet equal the pass or come bet as a right bettor, and equal the payoff on a don't pass or don't come bet.

Standoff — A tie, nobody wins. Also called a **Push**.

Stickman — Casino employee who controls the dice with a hooked stick, calls the game and controls the proposition bet area.

Toke or **Tip** — A gratuity either given or bet for the dealer.

Unit — Bet size used as a standard of measurement.

Working — Designation that a bet is on or in play.

Wrong Bettor — Players betting that the dice won't pass. Don't pass and don't come bettors.

Yo-Leven — Slang term for the roll of an 11.